Life in God's NOW

Life in God's NOW
The Sacrament of the Present Moment

Jean Pierre de Caussade's
Self-Abandonment to Divine Providence
for everyone

Elizabeth Ruth Obbard

Illustrated by the authoress

New City

First published in 2012
in Great Britain by
New City

© 2012 Elizabeth Ruth Obbard

Graphic and Cover design by Hildebrando Moguiê

British Cataloguing in Publication Data:
A catalogue reference to this book is available
from the British Library

ISBN 978-1-905039-11-1

Typeset in Great Britain by
New City, London

Printed and bound in Malta by Gutenberg Press

For Peter

'With God all things are possible'

CONTENTS

INTRODUCTION

Jean Pierre de Caussade, the author of the classic which came to be known as *Self-Abandonment to Divine Providence,* was born in Toulouse at the end of the seventeenth century. He joined the Jesuits in his home town at the age of eighteen and made his final vows in 1708. Between 1731 and 1749 de Caussade, who was known as a good preacher, was directing a retreat house in Nancy. While there, he undertook the spiritual direction of the Visitation nuns of that city along with his other work. The nuns made notes of the conferences de Caussade gave them, and these form the basis of the present book. However, the conferences were not published in book form for a wider readership until 1860, more than a hundred years later. Until then they were merely circulating in hand-written copies among the sisters of various convents.

De Caussade's classic was eventually edited and published by the Jesuit Henri Ramiere, who gave it the title with which it would be henceforth known: *Self-Abandonment to Divine Providence.* The book, as it first appeared in print, also included several abbreviations, additions and alterations from having been copied and circulated by hand over so many years. For it is worth repeating that this text was not designed to be a book at all. It was merely a compilation of a number of conferences given over the years to the Sisters of the Visitation who found them stimulating and helpful.

What Is Abandonment?

In de Caussade's view abandonment is a complete handing over of the self to God, finding in each moment the presence of God and the guiding hand of God's providence. It is a dynamic surrender that includes both active work and passive acceptance of what comes along. De Caussade's other original term 'The Sacrament of the Present Moment' refers to God's coming to us at each moment, as really and truly as God is present in the Sacraments of the Church: 'outward signs of inward grace'. In other words, in each moment of our lives God is present under the signs of what is ordinary and mundane. Only those who are spiritually aware and alert discover God's presence in what can seem like nothing at all. This keeps us from thinking and behaving as if only grand deeds and high flown sentiments are 'Godly'. Rather, God is present equally in the small things of life as in the great. God is there in life's daily routine, in dull moments, in dry prayers... There is nothing that happens to us in which God cannot be found. What we need are the eyes of faith to discern God as God comes at each moment – truly present, truly living, truly attentive to the needs of each one.

The Sources of de Caussade's Teaching

De Caussade's teaching is said to be based on that of Augustine, John of the Cross and Francis de Sales. That is certainly correct, but it has even deeper roots than this. It was for de Caussade a contemporary way of reiterating the long held monastic adage: *age quod agis* – 'Do what you are doing.' In other words, real and responsible living depends on living in the present, doing well what we are doing NOW. It is only when we begin to take this adage seriously that we realize how much we tend to live in the past or in the future. We think about what we have done or said or accomplished. We go over conversations and meetings in our minds and replay the old tapes of anger and hurt or praise and acclaim. Conversely we are thinking about what we shall do later on when the present task is completed. In other words we are not living to the full in the present. We do not actually live the moment we are in but the moments that have passed or the moments we hope will be coming later on. It is possible to live in such a manner that we do not actually LIVE our lives. We do not really listen to the birdsong, to the prayer we are saying, to the book we are reading, to the friend we are speaking to... Yes, we are there in body but not fully present in spirit. We are not PRESENT to the PRESENT.

Giving ourselves to the moment we are in, finding God in life's NOW is a discipline that we find almost impossible, simple as it sounds. The same teaching has been taken up once more in Eckhart Tolle's modern classic *The Power of Now*. Here again, Tolle has not really discovered something new, he has rediscovered the wisdom of the past, known by the monastics, by de Caussade and by other saints. St Thérèse of Lisieux could write towards the end of her own short life that, while once she had desired suffering, now abandonment was her only guide. At each moment she was ready to accept from God's hands whatever joy or sorrow God wished to give her. And because of this she was always happy deep down, for she had learned to want whatever God wanted her to have moment by moment.

The Sisters of the Visitation

It is worth remembering as we read de Caussade that these chapters on abandonment were originally given as talks to Visitandine nuns. The Order of the Visitation, founded by St Francis de Sales and St Jane Frances de Chantal, was designed to be an Order willing to accept women who often could not find a place in other convents because they were older, widowed, or had indifferent health. In a time when physical austerity was considered a *sine qua non* of a fervent religious life, the Visitation offered an alternative. Bodily penances were minimal, instead there were a number of practices designed to foster gentleness of spirit, kindness, a measured austerity that made the sisters compassionate towards each other, ready to accept dispensations to the Rule where necessary. The sisters might eat meat, sleep later than nuns of other Orders, forego harsh penance.

But their real penance was to accept graciously the pinpricks of community living, of constantly changing tasks, of a day made up of small things rather than great deeds.

De Caussade in his teaching therefore hones in upon the 'littleness' and 'ordinariness' that was the daily ambience of the Visitandine sisters. There was for them no taxing apostolate of nursing or teaching, no night Office or excessive fasting. There was just the discipline or daily routine in which God must be found. And of course this is where most of us, indeed all of us, have ultimately to find God. God is NOW and God is HERE, otherwise God is 'NOWHERE'. If God is not found in the here and now we will not find him in musings about the future or futile regrets over the past.

The Concept of Personal Vocation

Unlike ourselves, God does not look for and praise great and heroic deeds unless they are specifically asked of us. What God wants is the handing over of ourselves and our lives in complete trust, with confidence in God's mercy and God's care, so that we can become a living image of Jesus in the world of today.

De Caussade is at pains to point out that each of us has a vocation that is ours alone. If we do not do what God wants us to do there is no one else who can take our place. Let us be glad then that we are called as unique persons, with lives that are guided

14

by God's providence. In this way we reach our own personal fulfilment as parts of a greater whole.

Our most fervent prayer must always be 'Your will be done.' There is no greater gift we can give God than this surrender of self. With it God can make of our poor lives a song of praise to his glory. Without it all we might do of our own accord is worth nothing.

Note

This rendering of de Caussade's *Self-Abandonment to Divine Providence* is based on Kitty Muggeridge's translation of the original text without additions or accretions, and published by Fount under the title *The Sacrament of the Present Moment.*

LET IT BE DONE TO ME AS YOU HAVE SAID

1

HOW GOD SPEAKS
AND HOW WE MUST LISTEN

God still Speaks

God speaks to us today just as God spoke to people long ago. In those early days there was no need of spiritual directors promoting special methods of prayer and rules of life.

People were less sophisticated then. They realized that God's will was made known to them moment by moment as their day unfolded. It is the same today if only we listen and are ready to hear.

The Example of Mary

When the angel addressed Mary she replied 'Let it be done to me as you have said.' (Luke 1:38)

This reply summed up all the teaching of Mary's ancestors, which was contained in a simple and direct commitment to doing God's will, however that will was manifested in daily life.

Such simple words: 'Let it be done,' and how they show Mary's simplicity of soul!

What better words could anyone have on their lips and in their hearts than 'Thy will be done.'

Of course, Mary was being asked for something quite tremendous, but that would have been immaterial if she had not already been attuned to the will of God.

Whatever she was doing she was disposed to worship God and recognize God at work.

She knew that all she was asked to do or suffer at each moment was God's gift, something concrete and not mere dreams and wishes.

And so she was ready when the angel came to her with a special request. Just as she had been ready to do God's will in her whole life up to this moment.

The grace of God overshadowed Mary. And that shadow was nothing other than acceptance of the demands, duties and sufferings of each moment.

Just as a shadow can hide things from clear view, so God's will is not always clearly visible. We have, like Mary, to know God present in faith, and accept the Divine Will as it comes to us, often in shadow and darkness.

The angel may have left Mary, but the Holy Spirit never left her. And apart from this exceptional moment the gospels show Mary's life as ordinary. Nothing marks her out from other women of her own time and place.

She visits her relative, Elizabeth, as others do.

Like others, she goes to Bethlehem for the census where she gives birth to Jesus in poverty.

She lives quietly with her husband and son in Nazareth, working for a living.

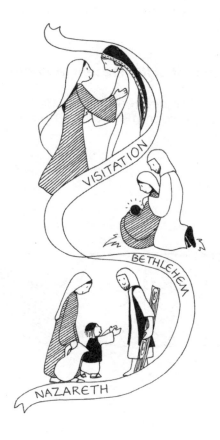

But what is the real bread that nourishes Mary and Joseph?

It is the bread of faith in God's will, hidden under the ordinary events of every day.

What is seen is ordinary. What is unseen is the fact that God is fulfilling the Divine purpose in and through their lives.

The Sacrament of the Present Moment

God's will is the heavenly bread that nourishes the angels. It is the sacrament of the present moment – life's NOW.

And where can we find this treasure?

It is there for us everywhere and always because the present moment is always with us.

In whatever our life consists the will of God is present, coming to us moment by moment.

Holiness is not something strange, difficult to find or far away.

Holiness is in the here and now of our own life.

No one needs directors, methods, rules if they follow this path.

Some people take pleasure in exercising control over others, while these others are always seeking advice.

All this is unnecessary.

If we look at the Old Testament the will of God was evident in all that happened in the lives of the Patriarchs and Prophets. There were no spiritual directors then. God was the only director through the events of a person's life.

It is the same for us.

Holiness is simple, not complicated.

Holiness is right here. Holiness is in life's NOW.

LIVING IN GOD

GOD LIVING IN US

2

JOURNEYING TOWARDS
SELF-SURRENDER

God in the Soul and the Soul in God

There are two ways of journeying belonging to two different times in our lives.

There is a time when we live in God.

And there is a time when God lives in us.

When we live in God we must explore carefully every means that will lead to Divine union.

God remains beside us as guide and friend, and we must follow the paths laid out for us by attentive reading, and evaluating our lives and ideas.

But when God lives in us there are no longer any clear plans or marked paths. We become like a child who can be led anywhere and sees only what is pointed out.

Often we are left in darkness, with no support other than God.

No matter how we feel, at this point we can only wait in hope, calm and untroubled, until God takes over and fulfils all our desires.

We may seem useless, but that is not the case.

People like this are so surrendered to God that nothing can disturb them, least of all what others may think.

When we live in God we can affect others just by being, even though we ourselves may not be aware of our virtues.

Like Jesus, Mary and Joseph we wait upon God's providence with no outward signs of living in an extraordinary manner.

God can take everything from us that pleases others and gains us human praise for, as with Jesus, the Divine life is hidden under an unprepossessing exterior. We are so completely given to God that God's will alone matters.

And so we follow the duty of each moment without hesitation, willing all that God wills, being all God wants us to be. This is the heart of the mystical journey.

Obedience to God's Time

Obedience to what God asks of us in life's NOW is the way in which we practise obedience to God's will.

We walk along the path looking neither to right nor left, doing what has to be done NOW and leaving the rest to God's providence.

People tend to think that those who love and serve God should take on extra devotions and rules, and shine in the eyes of those around them.

This is an error. <u>Giving ourselves to God does not mean doing lots of extra things. It means doing well what we have to do, and remaining in peace.</u>

God will put in our way the people who can give us the help we need to keep going.

<u>Let us know how to wait upon God's time rather than making plans of our own.</u>

3

HOW AND WHY WE SHOULD SURRENDER OURSELVES TO GOD

Give God the Freedom to Decide

Feelings are no gauge of progress, ultimately the duty of the present moment is what matters.

Attention to the present may make us act in one way or another, not because our reason tells us to do something but because we are attentive to the grace of God coming to us through many channels.

When we really want to walk with God we discover that we can do nothing except travel along the path in trust, having God alone as our guide. And God is often present to us only in the darkness of faith.

Accepting Suffering

Nobody likes bitter medicine, but when the doctor prescribes it we must take it, and trust that we will recover our health.

In the same way, bitter medicine from God has to be taken without fear of being poisoned. We may not swallow it gladly or easily, but take it we must.

Bitterness and suffering have to be accepted in faith as sent by God. But we do not feel very heroic about it, especially when we make a face taking this medicine and don't seem to be brave at all.

We feel so remote from the saints and their wonderful example of generosity. And yet, if we do what has to be done, in that is our true glory and destiny, even though we feel so totally inadequate.

God hides in order to increase our faith, as Jesus was unrecognized by Mary Magdalen in the garden of the Resurrection, even though she had earlier sat at his feet.

A Prayer for Light

O Divine Lord,
make us ready to seek you where we can
truly find you:
in solitude, in prayer, in obedience, in suffering,
in the service of others,
and in leaving aside all that might displease you.
Why are we always trying to find you where
you are not,
and not finding you where you really are?
What a foolish lot of folk we are.
Here you are in life's NOW
and we are looking for you somewhere else!
Give us light and strength to follow your path
and to trust in your leading.

GOD IS PRESENT IN OUR LITTLENESS

4

THE MYSTERY
OF DIVINE PROVIDENCE

God in the Ordinary

God is present even in our littleness and inadequacy.
Intelligence and great deeds are not the heart of
surrender.

Wide horizons, sure ground and solid rock are only
found in doing God's will in the midst of ordinary life.

We do what has to be done and leave it at that.
There is a sense of not knowing where we are going,
or what we are doing, because we can often feel so
helpless.

All we can do is to walk along one step at a time.

Eternity is already with us because eternity consists
in love, and love is embraced by us in the duties and
sufferings of the present.

Behind every cloud the sun is shining; so God is
there behind the clouds of suffering even when we
are not aware of the Divine presence.

We have to be light as a feather, fluid as water, innocent as a child, responding to each movement of grace as if we were a balloon floating along in the air currents, or like molten metal filling whatever vessel God pours us into.

Everything turns out for the best when we give ourselves unreservedly to God. All things work together for good for those who love God.

LIGHT · FLUID · RESPONSIVE

The Importance of Faith

Since we know that <u>God is responsible for everything
except sin</u> we must have great courage and great
confidence in this truth.

<u>Joy flows from unshakeable trust.</u>
     <u>Whatever God sends us we must learn to want and
welcome, for faith reaches out to grasp the hand of
God in everything</u>.
     When we know by faith that God is good, we can
<u>trust God absolutely.</u> Faith always lives in God, and
finds in God courage and joy to meet all of life's trials
and sufferings.

Don't give in to various 'illnesses' that sap inner strength. (Real illness that needs proper treatment is not what I am speaking of here). Cowardice makes much of small ailments, whereas strength of mind can uphold a frail constitution. Don't go under too easily! March on fearlessly!

We have to forget ourselves and our little aches and pains so that our real beauty and character can be tempered, refined, strengthened, and so shine out.

Discovering God in the midst of life demands faith.

Following and surrendering to God is how we exercise that faith. Let God do what God likes with us so that we become strong and fearless in love.

34

5

FAITH NOT SIGHT

The Gift of the Heart

We must want to give God our heart.

If we cannot manage that we must want to want it.

Good intentions can make up for weakness, for God does not ask of us extraordinary things.

Giving God our heart is to give God our freedom and our love. Anyone can do this. Surrender is the key to everything, a surrender lived out in daily life.

God doesn't ask the same things of each of us. God asks according to our nature and our gifts.

✳ We must be content to be who we are and to find in our own life the traces of God's care and God's providence.

The Primacy of Love

As soon as we are willing, love comes to take
possession of our hearts.

Love always wins through. It is invincible.

Pray for a pure heart, a single-hearted heart that knows how to see God in all that transpires, a heart where God dwells and where love is paramount.

Run along the way of love, don't just Walk!
    Love unlocks our true potential, it fosters holiness in everything, no matter how we feel. It gives hope of everlasting life. It teaches us lessons in and through all that we do.

... RUN ALONG THE WAY OF LOVE

6

WITH GOD THE LOSER WINS

Loving God for Godself

If help is given unknowingly, will there not be a greater gratitude when all is made clear?

With God, the more we seem to lose the more we gain.

The more God takes away from us the more God gives on the spiritual level.

A heart that is pure sees everything from the right angle – God's angle.

A real musician is so in tune with the music that, even without thinking about structure and composition, the musician's melodies have a touch of perfection about them.

When we are experienced in holiness we are like a good musician, everything that is done is done in tune with God and God's will as if it were second nature.

Thinking much gives way to loving much, a love that is natural and unforced. In fact we do not even realize that God is making music in our lives. We feel barren and hard, going on in faith alone. And yet, as we are attuned to God's will, the music plays on in the silence.

God Lives in Us

God hides in our hearts like a seed planted in the earth, a seed which in due course brings forth all kinds of flowers and fruits that we ourselves are unaware of.
We give shade and nourishment to others rather than feeding and adorning ourselves.

Let us nourish ourselves secretly on the leaves of grace like a little silkworm caterpillar in its cocoon, weaving silk that rulers would be proud to wear!

In the end God's transforming power will give us wings to fly up to heaven like a butterfly, our true self revealed and perfected in whatever form God has destined for us.

7

THE MYSTERY OF GRACE

What Is Grace?

Grace is God's will at work in us.

We don't need to learn a lot of theology to live out this truth. People who want to explain everything theoretically are like sick doctors trying to cure patients who are perfectly healthy!

Doing God's will in the day to day of life means being like patients who take a prescribed medicine without knowing how it works. All that is known is that they get better.

If you are thirsty – drink! It's no use reading books about drinking – that won't quench your thirst!

When we long for holiness, thinking about holiness and reading about holiness isn't the answer.

To be holy we must accept all that God sends us and all God requires of us moment by moment.

When we follow the Divine will we are in tune with grace; thus our souls will grow and flourish whether we can account for what is happening or not.

Making Room for Jesus

Doing God's will in life's NOW brings Jesus into our hearts.

If reading is the duty of the moment then read; if praying is the duty of the moment then pray; if working then work: and so on... Don't spend hours trying to decide what God is asking. Just do it!

Doing the Divine will makes the Divine present to us and within us.

Doing God's will unites us to God; there is no other way to union.

Let us respect God's leading and realize that not all of us are led along the same path. There is no place for rivalry, only respect for the uniqueness of each one.

If we tune into God's plans we will be safely nourished by good plain bread rather than fancy cake.

Let us acknowledge our own poverty and rely on God to give us what we need. We will be provided for, that is certain.

44

8

THE GIFT OF SELF

What We Have to Do

'Sacrifice a just sacrifice and hope in the Lord' (Psalm 4:8) said the psalmist.

That means that the only sure foundation of a spiritual life is to put ourselves wholly, body and soul, into God's hands.

We have to forget ourselves in order for God to become our joy, and for God's pleasure and glory to be the object of all our desires.

Be happy that God is God. Be happy to do all that God asks without questioning or drawing back from making a complete surrender of self.

The Ways in which God Uses Us

God uses us in two ways:
1) When we act on our own initiative.
2) When we let God act through us.

To act on our own initiative is to seek to do what God wants. To act on God's initiative means being open to God's inspirations.

Surrender makes both forms of action possible. It

entails a complete commitment to doing God's will in the present moment.

God wants us NOW.

God will show us the Divine will NOW.

Our part is to live in life's NOW so that God can take complete possession of our hearts, not at some time in the distant future but right NOW in the present moment.

The present is a present from God where God is found.

Open that present and find God in the simplicity of a pure heart that wants only what God wants.

The Place of Suffering

What we do is not as important as what God does.

God teaches us more through life's pains and sufferings than through ideas.

Ideas are just that – ideas. They have no substance in themselves, whereas love is practical and personal.

Love knows how to bear, believe, hope and endure all things for the love of Christ.

49

We have to know how to 'care and not to care' about what God sends. We will receive what we need to become holy; not necessarily what we have decided in advance will help us to holiness.

Being human we naturally feel our human poverty, so we must trust in God's mercy, not mystical gifts. God's word alone is our guide. If we want nothing but the Divine will we must be willing to be nothing in our own eyes and in the eyes of others.

Saying our 'Yes'

Saying 'Yes' to God demands both activity and passivity - doing and accepting.
    We must do all God asks.
    We must accept all God sends.

Doing what we must do is to act with simplicity and safety. We can then go ahead without undue concern about theology or high-flown thinking. God teaches us on a deeper level than that.

However, remaining in the present moment takes great courage. To sing the song of abandonment, no matter what storms are raging around us, makes us like Jesus.

Jesus walked the way of his passion and cross in loving obedience to the Father, even though it meant being treated in a way that was totally opposed to his human dignity.

Jesus marched on undaunted, and so should we. God alone matters and doing God's will is how we show that God matters most.

Weaving the Tapestry of our Life

When a tapestry is being stitched the stitches are made on the reverse side of the canvas. The final pattern is only revealed when the stitching is completed and the design seen in all its beauty right side up.

Surrendering ourselves to God moment by moment is like making a stitch on the reverse side of a tapestry. One stitch at a time is one more step towards completing the full design that we shall see only in eternity.

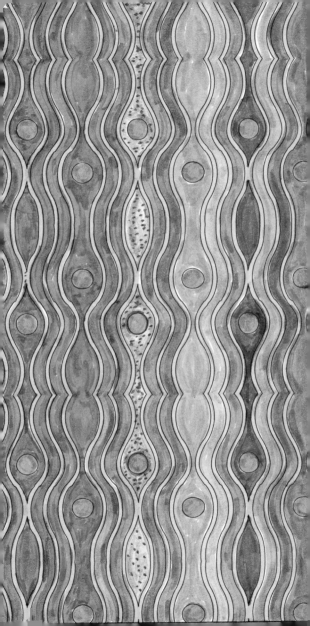

Our tapestry is made moment by moment, stitch by stitch. There is nothing here outside the capacity of anyone.

Fidelity to duty is within the reach of all, and on it is built the most perfect holiness.

Doing God's Will

Our duty consists in two things:

1) What God asks of us as members of the human race.

2) What God asks of us specifically because of our own particular calling.

No one lives exactly the same kind of life as another, although there may be similarities.

There is nobody else quite like me. God's mercy and grace are available to me as the unique person I am.

It is no use comparing myself with the saints.

Sometimes lives of holy people seem quite outside the possibilities offered to me. That is because I am different and live in a different life situation, with different graces and gifts.

Yet as God gives us human life and all we need for our bodily existence like air, water, light, so God gives us all that we need for our spiritual flourishing.

If we give ourselves to God we can be sure we will receive all that is necessary to grow in holiness.

Our daily duties are given to us at each moment. All we have to do is respond with generosity.

The saints did God's will.
That is the secret of sanctity, and that is possible for us too.

BLOOM WHERE GOD PLANTS YOU

God Is at Work

God is weaving the tapestry of our lives, or in another metaphor, working like a painter one brushstroke at a time, or a carver one chisel mark at a time.

We must let God be God for us without being overly concerned about the finished product.

Doing God's will takes effort.

We can't just lie back and expect God to do everything for us. We must do our part too. <u>If God inspires us to act then we must act</u>. If not then we must be content to accept peacefully whatever God sends. Either we weave our tapestry or let God work on us with the divine chisel or paintbrush.

What we actually do doesn't count as much as the love with which we do it. Doing great and wonderful things isn't the nub of the matter. If we act as God wills then we attain perfection, whether great deeds are asked of us or not.

Finding True Peace

✳ Self-discipline is the first essential for true peace. We can't attain peace if we are driven here and there by forces that we make no effort to control.

The second essential is self-surrender and abandonment.

The third necessity is a humble heart, ready to respond willingly to whatever God asks.

And so that we may not lose our way God sends us those who can best help us along the path. Wise guides enable us to discern how much freedom and how much constraint is applicable in our own case.

Dreaming about a holiness that manifests itself in heroic deeds is useless if God does not ask these of us. We must resolve firmly to respond to the inspirations of the Holy Spirit and do what we can in our daily life situation.

This means being fully present to what we are doing NOW. Suffering what we are called upon to suffer NOW.

The outward situation doesn't have to change. The heart alone needs to be rightly ordered, then the rest will fall into place.

WISE GUIDES CAN HELP

9

GOD'S WILL
AND THE SACRAMENT
OF THE PRESENT MOMENT

God's Leading

We must have great confidence in God's leading
and God's providence.

In accordance with our faith and our love, we
will discover the riches present in each successive
moment.

God's power and strength are there to help us
whenever we call on them.

Recognizing God's Presence

If we know that we are meeting a King in disguise we
treat him differently from an ordinary person because
we are aware of his dignity and status.

In the same way, if we realize that God comes to us
disguised in the duties of the present moment, we
receive everything that happens with equal honour

and delight. <u>Whether the moment brings grief, suffering or joy on the natural level, God is present.</u>

God appears to us in the most humble disguises.

Look at Bethlehem – God lying on straw in a manger, trembling and crying like any other baby.

Surely the people of Bethlehem would have taken notice of a prince born in a palace. But here they saw nothing to commend the Child to them.

Yet if we ask Mary, Joseph and the Magi what they think, we would discover that they see in this poverty and humility something that strikes them as glorious and adorable.

The eyes of faith are what make the difference, not the outward surroundings.

To adore Jesus at the Transfiguration is not so difficult. To adore Jesus on the cross demands all the faith we can muster.

To discover Jesus in great things that bring us notice and praise is not as hard, and does not call on our spirit of faith, as much as finding Jesus in small and trivial things where he is also present, but in humble disguise.

Mary was ready to follow Jesus to Calvary.

Everything natural must have said to her 'God is not here' yet she went on, faithful to the end. She remained at the foot of the cross when all the apostles had fled away. She recognized her son beneath the bruises, spittle, wounds and cries of pain. What greater faith could there be?

The same degree of faith is asked of us when we must recognize the presence of God in what is hard and demanding.

Jesus has gone before us. We have only to follow faithfully.

The Living Word

As God's written word in the Bible is full of mystery, so is God's word mysterious when revealed in what God does now.

God's words and works are like a dark valley with faith flowing in its depths, or like dim rays from a remote sun.

All that we read of in the Bible, strange as it may sometimes seem, is a message from God, a ray from the sun.

All that has happened in history is likewise a message from God to which we may be blind, until we stop trying to reason everything out and walk in the way of faith.

Often instead of finding God in the Bible, in history, in our own personal life story, we see only tragedy and chance, rather than God's providence. Only the eyes of faith enable us to see truly.

Faith here – glory hereafter. There is no other way to discover God. In this the Holy Spirit enlightens and teaches us.

If we want wisdom rather than an accumulation of bare facts we must allow God's Spirit to lead us into a rapture such as the saints experienced. Rapture like this takes us out of ourselves and our own limited way of seeing, and into the Divine way of faith where we see God continually at work in all that has happened, is happening, and will happen in the future.

God is here in history and in our lives. God is always at work. Every moment is a revelation, a word from God if only we allow ourselves to become aware of that fact.

Saints are those who had a faith that stayed firm through all the trials of life.

Visions, mystical graces and so on, are not what make the saints saints – only faith.

Real faith doesn't need signs and wonders, rather it finds proof of God's providence in life's day-to-day happenings.

Many who are real saints are never known on earth. They are hidden beneath an unprepossessing exterior and will shine only in heaven.

Me – a Saint?

If I only sip from the water of God's life I will remain thirsty. If I drink deeply, then my thirst will be quenched.

In the same way, if I just try to be a saint by doing a little here and a little there I won't get anywhere fast. If I abandon myself to God wholeheartedly and generously I shall soon attain holiness.

There is no other secret to learn, except that of complete abandonment to God moment by moment.

Learning to see God at work in my own life is far more profitable than just reading about God's presence and work in the lives of other people, no matter how holy.

Jesus speaks to each one of us. The Holy Spirit is always present to us.

We don't have to crave martyrdom. We can die for God or live for God by accepting all that God sends us, and accepting it with love here and now.

I too can be a saint!

God's Grace Is Sufficient

God's grace is ever present in all that happens. It penetrates and pervades every pore of our being. It carries us along like a deep flowing current to which we have only to surrender ourselves.

Come, all who want God, learned or simple, and discover the map of the spiritual journey. Don't worry how others are walking.

Trust the way you yourself are called to follow and walk in it with confidence. God's grace will not fail you. Each one of us can bring God's message to others like the prophets of old. It is we who continue to write the book of God's words and works in the present day.

God doesn't put down the pen just because the official Scriptures are finished! We are the living books of the Holy Spirit still in the making.

Purity of Heart

It's no use looking elsewhere for inspiration if we don't have the wisdom that finds God in our own life.

Reading God's word is not enough. We have to be formed in the image of Jesus by the Spirit, and become a living word. Attaining that goal takes great purity of heart.

LIVING BOOKS

<u>Purity of heart means being content with our own lot in life.</u> We can waste a lot of time trying to think things out, tying ourselves in knots as if the way to God was complicated and difficult to decipher.

God wants to welcome us home like the prodigal son and feed us with solid food, not the airy-fairy ideas we tend to delight in.

The present moment tells us all we need to know. In the present moment God is present and active NOW.

The prayer Jesus gave us, the Our Father, sums up everything. We make God's kingdom a reality when we do the Divine will. In doing God's will we receive our daily bread, the measure of suffering and joy that God has chosen for us.

BLESSED ARE THE PURE IN HEART

Real wisdom doesn't concentrate on the paucity of what is felt. Rather it discerns how the heart is filled as the senses are emptied.

A pure heart, a wise heart, looks for fulfilment where alone it can be found – in God.

Heavenly Food for Heavenly People

The Israelites of old were fed with manna during their time in the desert; a heavenly food that came from the hand of God day by day, and according to the needs of each one.

It is useless to stuff ourselves greedily with accounts of the lives of the saints, tomes of spirituality, God-talk and so on, if we neglect the present moment in which is all the nourishment we need.

Other things can only be useful if they are according to God's present will. They are a means to an end, not an end in themselves.

Whatever God gives is what we must want to have.

Manna from heaven comes only a day at a time. Let us feed upon the will of God moment by moment and we shall not need to seek out other food of our own choosing.

Holiness is integral to belonging to God. If we want to be holy we must accept all that God sees fit to give us without tiring our minds with subtle reasoning.

What food can we eat if the food God gives seems tasteless? Do we know better than God what will nourish us? Surely not!

Revere God present in your heart NOW. You have all you need if you only trust in God's leading and feeding.

10

HOLINESS MEANS LOVING, SERVING AND OBEYING GOD IN ALL THINGS

All Is Well

Surrender to the will of God and you will be able to say in every circumstance 'It is the Lord!'

Faith tells us that God is tender and merciful. But God is also one who turns us like a potter turns clay on a wheel.

We must submit to all that happens knowing that ultimately 'All will be well.' We will be fashioned in the divine likeness if we surrender generously to God's working.

Using another image – be simple, straightforward, trusting, and God will bring the ship of your life into port.

Sail securely on the waves of God's will. Let God fill the wind in your sails. The Spirit takes over lives that are totally given to God in faith.

'Blessed are the pure in heart.' Have a heart that is attuned to God's will and you cannot go wrong, for God makes the Divine will known to us moment by moment, no matter what is happening in our lives.

Following our Star

People who are anxious about human plans like Herod, or the Pharisees that we meet in the gospels, are always troubled and ill at ease; whereas the Magi have only to follow the star, the Child Jesus has only to lie in his mother's arms.

Magi and Child are completely at peace. They don't have to fight evil. They just allow God to take over while they remain abandoned to the Divine will.

In this way souls become free, fearless, serene and detached, because they see the hand of God at work in everything.

They bless the Divine hand that gives them life, and they treat everyone with equal respect and gentleness as Jesus did.

This is something we learn, not from books, but from daily practice: doing what we have to do, loving those we are called upon to love, responding to the Spirit in freedom, joy and peace of heart.

What more could anyone desire?

What about Evil?

In the book of Daniel we read of a monster statue made of gold, bronze, iron and clay. That is what the world sometimes seems like – a great amalgam of all sorts of evil.

Each age has its own monsters and tyrants. There is war, disharmony, disunity... you name it, we have it!

The root of evil is a rejection of the order that originates in God. Yet history shows that evil can never have the last word. People intent upon evildoing may think they are invincible, but they are mistaken.

The monster of gold, bronze, iron and clay is ultimately nothing but a heap of glittering dust that the wind disperses in a moment.

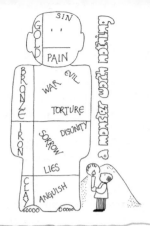

Evil may try us, but if we trust in God it can never come out on top. Faith is our winning weapon in the fight.

God brings good out of evil for those who trust, just as God builds the heavenly Jerusalem from the rubble of Babylon.

A pure heart finds God where God was thought to be absent.

Faith gives us light to see with the eyes of God rather than our own limited vision.

The chaos of evil cannot replace the order of God.

Carry on regardless of all else. Cling to God's will. Do what you have to do. Be humble and gentle. Then the truth will enlighten you and you will see with the eyes of God.

Beneath the outward appearance of an ordinary life the Virgin Mary shed over all things a shining, but invisible, glory. So shall we if, like her, we surrender to God through thick and thin, maintaining our peace and joy in all that befalls us.

11

THE DARK NIGHT OF FAITH

God Holds Us Safely

When we are clear about the way to go then it is
easy to walk as those who walk in the brightness of
day.

But there are also times when the way is dark and
obscure because God hides in the darkness of faith.

We have no cause to be afraid of the dark night of
faith.

Indeed, even though good and virtuous actions
can seem, and are, worthwhile, the heart at this stage
is more attracted to darkness and mystery, knowing
that God is present in it.

75

We must therefore surrender ourselves totally into the hands of God. We will be carried if God makes the path too dangerous and obscure for walking.

Don't be afraid! God will never desert you. Do what you have to do. Avoid all sin. Nothing more is asked.
   Beyond the shadows the light shines. Reasoning isn't any help. Only faith.

At this point we are led as if from behind. God is there holding us and urging us on, but we cannot see God's face and it is useless to try. We find the way by losing ourselves and welcoming the difficulties that come from life. Difficulties and darkness teach us things that we cannot learn in the light.

Carry on Carrying on

'All is well' must be our theme song, with its ending 'Glory be to God!'

Remember Abraham. The more Isaac worried about finding an animal to sacrifice, the more Abraham relied on God for everything. And sure enough, at the right time he was vindicated in his trust.

If we are walking in the light our songs will be light-hearted. If we are walking in darkness our songs will echo the state of our soul. What matters is to keep singing.

Prophets like Ezekiel and Jeremiah wept and lamented. Pessimism and optimism aren't different. They both come from the same source, and are two sides of the same coin.

Accept life's sorrows and pains and you will come through them to a deeper joy.

Walking the Way

Some people think that they have to do nothing. God will do it all for them.

They are badly mistaken if they reason in this manner.

In the Bible people weren't always serene and happy. They had to face pain and suffering. They had to cope with a God who seemed sometimes to lead them along difficult and unpredictable paths.

We have to surrender to a guide who takes us through unknown territory. No use consulting maps or asking others the way! We just have to trust our guide.

Each one of us is unique, no one is a carbon copy of anyone else, and the life and actions of each cannot be duplicated.

We are asked to incarnate the life of Jesus in our own life. But no one will do it in quite the same way.

JESUS LIVING IN MY OWN LIFE

We are each a new testament of Jesus living again in the world, just as in a garden each flower in a border is unlike any other. The only similarity is in the flowers' submission to the hand and design of the gardener.

'God's will be done.' That is the universal law we must follow. Doing God's will means acting at the right time and surrendering in darkness at other times.

Obedience is the key. Faith is the watchword. 'Blessed are those who have not seen and yet believe.'

Jesus still Lives

Jesus lives and works among us from the beginning of our lives until the end. Jesus lived on earth and still lives. The life of Jesus continues to this day in the lives of the saints and in our own poor lives too.

The good news of the gospel is made present in us. It gives Christ a thousand different faces, a thousand different ways of being.

Our family history helps us to understand something of our personal heritage; and in the same way, the story of salvation history helps us to understand more about who Jesus is and the promises he came to fulfil.

The Spirit must now write the life of Jesus in our own lives and the lives of those about us. The ink is still wet, the writing in progress. But the writing is in a language

we do not understand, and the paper is darker than the ink!

Twenty-six letters of the alphabet make words of astonishing variety. They express feelings, thoughts, actions... They fill volumes. In the same way God is writing numerous books, each one different, each one with its own meaning and story. But only faith enables us to open them and read what God is writing.

A Prayer for Understanding the Book of Life

Teach me, Holy Spirit, to read rightly the book
of my life. I will be your disciple and believe
what I cannot see.
That God speaks at every moment is enough,
the rest I take on trust.
Every letter written in the book of my life
has meaning and purpose.
I can only understand things dimly right now;
later I will know with certainty.
May Jesus live in my life now at every moment,
and let me recognize that truth by faith.
Write the book that is my life, Holy Spirit of God,
make it a continuation of the holy Scriptures.
Everything is holy, everything finds a place in you.
Give me eyes to see, ears to hear,
and a heart that believes.
Amen.

FOR FURTHER READING

Texts

De Caussade, Jean Pierre, *The Sacrament of the Present Moment*, Trans. Kitty Muggeridge, Fount 1981

De Caussade, Jean Pierre, *Self-Abandonment to Divine Providence*, Trans. Algar Thorold, Burns and Oates 1933

Related Reading

De Caussade, Jean Pierre, *On Prayer*, Trans. Algar Thorold, Burns and Oates 1949

De Caussade, Jean Pierre, *Letters*, Trans. Algar Thorold, Burns and Oates 1934

De Sales, Francis and Jane de Chantal, *Letters of Spiritual Direction*, Trans. Peronne

Marie Thibert VHM, *Classics of Western Spirituality* Series, Paulist 1988

Tolle, Eckhart, *The Power of Now*, Hodder and Stoughton 1999

INTRODUCING

JULIAN
WOMAN of NORWICH

ELIZABETH RUTH OBBARD

This book, beautifully illustrated by the author herself, introduces Julian to a wider readership by setting her in her own time and place and giving a selection of illustrated readings from Revelations of Divine Love. It is a book that will provide many hours of fruitful reflection.

ISBN: 978-1-905039-14-2
130 pp PB £7.50

Regina Goberna OSB
& Lourdes Viñas OSB

OUR FATHER
ST BENEDICT

A book of simple meditations accompanied by line drawings which follow St. Benedict in his discovery of the Gospel.

ISBN: 978-1-905039-06-7
127 pp PB £7.50

Elizabeth Ruth Obbard

THE CLOUD
OF UNKNOWING
for everyone

The author, herself a contemplative Carmelite, introduces the reader to this spiritual classic through her very accessible prose and simple, yet beautiful illustrations. Anyone who is attracted by the contemplative life, whilst living in the midst of our busy world, will find this little book a great help.

ISBN: 978-0-904287-97-4
88 pp PB   £5.95

Elizabeth Ruth Obbard

GOSPEL CHILDHOOD

The 'Little Way' of
St Therese of Lisieux for everyone

This little book really does take the reader to the heart of Therese's message. Simple, yet profound, and illustrated with the author's own drawings, this is a book to treasure, to read and re-read, each time discovering something new about Therese of Lisieux.

ISBN: 0-904287-94-7
96 pp PB £5.95

Elizabeth Ruth Obbard

St Teresa's
WAY OF PERFECTION
for everyone

The author of the ever popular
*Introducing Julian woman of
Norwich* has come up with
another gem in this simple
but profound guide to the
spirituality of St Teresa of Avila.
She takes the reader right to
the heart of the great Spanish
mystic's way to union with
God.

ISBN: 0-904287-78-5
94 pp PB £5.95

Elizabeth Ruth Obbard

**THE LIVING FLAME
OF LOVE**
of
St John of the Cross

This is the third in Elizabeth
Obbard's popular series of
spiritual biographies with a
difference. She is able to
communicate the amazing
depth of St John of the Cross's
spiritual experience in the
simplest of ways in this book,
beautifully illustrated by the
author herself.

ISBN: 0-904287-88-2
83 pp PB   £5.95